"The latest collaboration between Jason Baldinger and James Benger hits like perfect rock n' roll poetry dedicated to every bar regular who never thought anything of their thoughts and instead decided to light a cigarette. With images of winters too cold for human empathy and midwestern frustrations brought on because nothing wants to go right, Baldinger and Benger's latest is an excellent portrait of poetic working-class Americana. A fiery Whitman-esque yawp not meant for literary luminaries but for those who don't know how to define the fire within themselves."

 -Daniel W. Wright, author of *Love Letters from the Underground*

"In *This Still Life*, Jason Baldinger & James Benger return for a third masterful collaboration with Baldinger sending out his calls like a lone bird in the Rust Belt, waiting for Benger's answer in the Midwest. Two unique voices studying this span where "we only live a handful of days", finding the beauty in struggle & loss through fine-tuned lenses as time & place are travelled, observed, & recorded for any who come across this collection of musings in the future. "All this is temporary", so let's make our way to the stream or ocean & enjoy this moment before we resurface."

 -Tim Heerdink, author of *Somniloquy & Trauma in the Knottseau Well*

Also by Jason Baldinger:

The Whiskey Rebellion w/ Jerome Crooks (Six Gallery Press)
The Lady Pittsburgh (Speed and Briscoe Press)
The Lower Forty-Eight (Six Gallery Press)
The Studs Terkel Blues (Nightballet Press)
Fumbles Revelations (Grackle and Crow)
This Useless Beauty (Alien Buddha Press)
The Ugly Side of the Lake w/ John Dorsey (Nightballet Press)
The Better Angels of our Nature (Kung Fu Treachery Press)
Blind into Leaving (Analog Submission Press)
A Threadbare Universe (Kung Fu Treachery Press)
The Afterlife if a Hangover (Stubborn Mule Press)
The Nu Profit$ of P/O/E/T/I/C Di$chord: *And Even if we Did, So What!?* (OAC Book w/ Damian Rucci, Shawn Pavey, Nathaniel Stolte
A History of Backroads Misplaced: Selected Poems 2010-2020 (Kung Fu Treachery)
Little Fires Hiding (Kung Fu Treachery Press)
Everyone's Alone Tonight (Kung Fu Treachery Press)

Also by James Benger:

Flight 776 (LAB 52)
Jack of Diamonds (LAB 52)
As I Watch You Fade (EMP)
You've Heard it All Before (GigaPoem)
Against the Dark (with Tyler Robert Sheldon) (Stubborn Mule Press)
The Park (Kelsay Books)
Things Have Changed (Dark Particle Press)
From the Back (Spartan Press)
Misfits in the Front Row (with Sarah Worrel)
(Kung Fu Treachery Press)
Little Fires Hiding (Kung Fu Treachery Press)
Everyone's Alone Tonight (Kung Fu Treachery Press)

This Still Life

Poems by
Jason Baldinger and James Benger

Kung Fu Treachery Press
Rancho Cucamonga, CA

Copyright © Jason Baldinger, James Benger, 2022
First Edition: 1 3 5 7 9 10 8 6 4 2
ISBN: 978-1-952411-96-0
LCCN: 2022934418

Cover image: Jon Dowling, Jason Baldinger
Interior image: Jason Baldinger
Author photos: Michele Revay, Sarah Minges
All rights reserved. No part of this publication may be reproduced or transmitted in any form or by any means, electronic or mechanical, including photocopying, recording or by info retrieval system, without prior written permission from the author.

Acknowledgments:

Jason would like to thank: James for continually writing beautiful poems, Jon Dowling, Rob Gray, Jason Ryberg, John Dorsey, Victor Clevenger, Bob Pajich, Alanna Miles, Scott Silsbe et al.

James would like to thank Jason for continuing to let me write books with him, Jason Ryberg at Kung Fu Treachery Press for repeatedly giving our books a home, the members of *365 Poems in 365 Days* for putting up with me constantly pummeling them with early drafts, and Dad, Hannah, Milo, and Felix.

Some of the poems in this book were previously published in various forms in *365 Days, Vol. 3, Winedrunk Sidewalk, As It Ought to Be, River Dog, Gasconade Review, Anti-Heroin Chic, Rusty Truck, Rye Whiskey Review, Green Panda Press, Mad Swirl, Live Nude Poems, Rustbelt Review*

Table of Contents

another monochrome day / 1

The Color of Now / 3

hymn to groundhog day / 5

The Ritual / 7

for the little conemaugh / 9

Horizon / 11

an existential fuck / 13

Disrepair / 16

in a lonely place / 18

Casual Incantation / 20

kings bridge armory may 6, 1919 / 22

1942 / 24

when hope is on life support / 25

Sunday / 27

hymn to thrift store ties / 30

Trajectory / 33

our great and wasted hours / 35

Anonymous / 36

say hello anywhere / 38

Inanimate Tears / 40

panther hollow lubrication / 42

Cinder / 44

the eyes of the world / 46

Sensory / 48

civic arena march 7, 1984 / 50

Blood / 52

where are you now benny santiago / 54

Last Night's Whisper / 57

I can't make this akron / 59

Twelve Bar / 61

once I was / 63

Claude's Brush / 65

working poor pretend / 67

Twelve Points Shuffle / 68

regular and subtle as god / 69

Tomorrow's Chance / 71

spook the horse / 72

Another Cold One / 74

our temporary time / 76

Ocean / 78

ask the dunes / 79

Stream / 81

'Tis a sigh that is wafted across the troubled wave,
'Tis a wail that is heard upon the shore
'Tis a dirge that is murmured around the lowly grave
Oh! Hard times come again no more.

-Stephen Foster, "Hard Times Come Again No More"

It's never too early to throw in the towel,
but it's always too late to die with dignity.

-Mishka Shubaly, "Your Stupid Dreams"

This Still Life

another monochrome day

at the dog leg light
with the ghost
house, memories
of prohibition era
bathtub gin leaking
fumes into an ever
darkening sky

pillsbury sign
skirmish of endless rain
noise spills out of
the horoscope lounge
another soulful strut
drunk takes wings
glides past george aiken's
while corner horns
street lights blow
along to a four beat

the coffee shop
clings to a revolving
door of hangovers
it seems every soul
is wider this morning

saucers of the moon
lost in the iris

of this old neighborhood
song, I swear
I'm breathing again
fingers tap on steering
wheel, light blinks green
hand spun turns
chooglin'
another split atom
another monochrome day

-Baldinger

the color of now

midnight puddles reclaim
the uneven broadway intersection
harkening all to observe
the desolate isolation
that this year has
bestowed upon the uptown

just south
the greasy spoon
gave up to mcdonald's
but you can still get
ice melt at the 7-11
if you're in a pinch for traction

the old man
who's probably
not as old as he looks
under the streetlights
holds a cardboard sign
and his dignity
close to his chest

there are uneven railways
not far from here
threatening to
turn anyone's night long
protracted lessons in patience

that may've been a car backfiring
or a gunshot
or fireworks
celebration
and decay
and violence
have become synonymous

the wind kisses a promise
of eternal january
and the old man on the corner
makes me think of the statue
out front of the
korean war memorial

the windshield goes the green of
all those imagined summers

-Benger

hymn to groundhog day

this café is contrary
a strange anomaly in a land of diners
wallpaper bricks with watercolor mustangs
one calendar, two posters of the hulk
one hulk decal on the cooler
I wonder about the calendar to quality ratio
an equation mastered in *blue highways*
then wonder how many hulk posters equal a
    calendar

the waitress says her son raises groundhogs
I don't know what to say
maybe she's fucking with me
I look deep in the hulk's eyes
this year he has forty-two groundhogs
I say, *that sure is a lot of groundhogs*

bessemer tunnels and carbon snow
a few towns away
my mother's family settled in the 1850's
dropping the A and E
dropping the family crest
marrying into a family with a township named
after them

a yellow sign juts from the snow in surrender
I miss the america I grew up in
I want to believe this is a statement
on a widening gap in equality

on the erosion of class
on the working persons giving everything away
on the ways we allow government to fail
in not mandating social responsibility

instead, it's another absurd conservative screed
about the good old days that never were
times when people went to church
family values happened and abortions didn't

the stop signs have addendums
one says *stop touching me*
another *stop, hump me*
the last, *stop and dance*
these winter messages so conflicted

I hunt frozen snakes along the kiskiminetas
here in the bleak of february
I fill myself with enough gray
to crush the restlessness that grows each snow

punxsutawney
ten hours after the groundhog
he saw his shadow
so did this town

there is no evidence this civilization
still tries to understand weather
through the eyes of animals

-Baldinger

the ritual

he would get up early
of a weekday morning
take himself out to the
back of his three acres
the last bit wooded
sit himself in an
aluminum lawn chair
sight down the crooked barrel
and shoot

he claimed for the deer
he never seemed to bag
the deer no one else ever saw

but i'm still not convinced
he wasn't shooting at god
or his past
or his future
trying to paint the morning
in buckshot
trying to blast back to start

he would talk about the rails
and the summer sun
about horses
and barbed wire
and shovels

he never touched on
the uncertainty
floating just under the
surface of his eyes
he never talked about the flowering dread
of a world that withdrew itself
seemingly more rapidly every day

when the wet would come
his cane would tell you
all you needed to know
shoving wood into the stove
unused prohibition stills
in the basement
each year covering the memories
the stories
in another coat of regret

after he was in the ground
i went out back
fired a rifle into the trees
it didn't help

-Benger

for the little conemaugh

this charmless winter
shy across asphalt miles
fresh snow melts morning

paul newman scratches
the neck of the dog
that tried to save you

it worked once

I pick factory bones
try to see
try to really see
you, I can't get
past the trauma

the dead eyes
of pretty blondes
waterfalls lurch across
the town square
wait out the last bus
wait out the city mission

there's a red lit sign
jesus saves
there's a pink sombrero
alone at a lunch counter

vintage owls
watch over
little conemaugh
I stand with them
on the mountain above
the trees break
another world vista
a hole in the earth

I see a burial party
come to cover you in mud
while that rain brown river
never dredged safe
rages in a concrete bed

this history is suspect
spit out debris
of capitalists
titans of industry
they whisper
it's only mud

it's only mud

-Baldinger

horizon

we stumble these backroads
of what once was
what might've been

there are worlds
universes
in the cracks of the pavement

rivers flow in the unblemished sky
a sky that if you squint
and try real hard
will tell you
sweet air is still out there
just not here

boot soles on ancient earth
those grains of dirt
hold more wisdom
more history
than any of us
could ever hope to know

shop windows threaten
distorted glimpses of ourselves
our true intentions
often too gruesome
to give face

behind clouds the sun is a joke
a notion of what others see
but not us
not now

we walk on
hope to find the hills
hope to find ourselves
hope to find anything
other than this

-Benger

an existential fuck

no way to keep dread down
I mean that existentially
I mean that physically
when I'm alone
my heart becomes
a separate entity
it tries its damndest
to leap from my throat
        from my chest

what leaves me stymied
is the grief, dying country
dying culture, dying economy
no surprises, moribund
corpulent, ossified are all
words for this republic then
now this republic of suffering

what leaves me stymied
is the grief, the numbers
of the dead daily
the lack of empathy
from the true believers
the manchurian candidates
their frothing protests
moloch be praised
moloch be praised

when I see friends
conversation teeters
we vacillate wildly
a little hope, a little dread
nothing for the pain
nothing for the anxiety

as we talk we pause
wait for traction again
the wheels of aching minds
what escapes is a sigh
heavy and weighted
a cry from our collective
organism brain
the force of will
to take another breath
to say another sentence
escapes us, wind rattles
through our teeth
on a page it might look
like ellipsis, like this
...
except longer
....
it can only be described
as an existential fuck

fffffuuuuuccccckkkkk
no force in a limp breeze
resignation at the hands

of this time escaping
lost between shores
of what's been, what's coming
of what's failed and what we hope for

I find comfort in camus
as I tread the water of now
I'll do my best to paraphrase

if life is ruled by death
we should ignore god
and fight like hell against it

-Baldinger

disrepair

he threw a wrench today

right across the workshop
where it took out any number of
various items from the pegboard
the red rage glowed luciferian
as tools clanged to concrete

he did everything right
everything goddamnit

but here he is
late at night
doing his best to
frankenstein back to life
a cobbled vacuum cleaner
because who could afford
anything new now

it was all right
it was all good
until it wasn't
and he's not sure
when the shift happened
but it did
and now he knows
he's in too deep

he thinks of the walnuts on grandpa's farm
how clean and pure they tasted
how precise
how delicate the procedure
of removing flesh from shell
how it never rained
or if it did
it wouldn't last

this dream was a lie
it might've been true
for someone somewhere sometime
but not now
not for him
maybe not ever
probably not ever

he goes over to the pegboard
methodically picks up his mess
carefully replacing each item
because that's the best he can do

-Benger

in a lonely place

bogart
draped in smoke
of a freshly lit cigarette
checks lines
on his face in the mirror
insides chewed up
he internalizes
the violence, the trauma
this world has done
everything to break him

gloria graham
could be mistaken
for being icy in hollywood
midnight. she understands
bogart's lines as she brushes
past him in the courtyard
she hadn't believed in love
at first sight…till now
she needs to process
her heart, she knows
she'll think for them both

mildred atkins yells help
santa monica boulevard
is where california falls
into the sea. maybe two

broken people can fall in love
with bodies hanging around
their necks, sometimes
it's only the loneliness
that keeps them from
spiraling out, light another
cigarette this was supposed
to be a love poem, I think

graham is on a plane
to new york, the ticket
cost her everything

nicolas ray
dead in an eyepatch
waits on sterling hayden's guitar

what happened to bogart
is unknown, black and white
photo lost swirls in seafoam
just a memory hushed
detritus floating under the pier

dust highlights, freefall
in projection over shadows
truth be told, we have lives
to forget, we span time
we live only a handful of days

-Baldinger

casual incantation

we act as though
any of this
precludes anything

our bones are stiffening
in this action of inaction
looking toward a future
that is not only
not guaranteed
but vastly unlikely

notions of meaning
are lost in lethargy
when reason to move
is shackled by a malicious
half-welcomed delirium
of blessedly cursed indecision

under prescribed lines of
inarticulate stirring
any notion of a last chance
is less than a fuzzy ghost
of an abstract concept

we pretend these are the moments
where we bide our time
straining our eyes

to see just over the edge
to the other side of the hill
where we force ourselves
to believe there's gold

because if we can't believe in
that mumbled magic
what the hell
can we believe in

-Benger

kings bridge armory may 6, 1919

we were so bloody tired
we could barely conjure emotion
the soldiers would pass
silver trays, ashen faces
we were machines
spooning food
little talk

our eyes blank
their eyes reflect
visions of the dead
light of their souls
barely strobe
perhaps this is all
perhaps this is all that's left

he wasn't gone
little more light
if only a little
the look on his face
maybe a crumbled smile

a red rose in the button
of his pocket. I, shocked
alive for a moment
some color in drab time
very possible I blush

suddenly exposed
suddenly acutely aware
of feeling once again
as if I forgot
we were human
for a second

this still life

my eyes drawn to color
his voice recognizes, gaunt
they were showered
in roses yesterday
everyone in the village
wanted to kiss
the heroes of the 77th
who were they to argue

I didn't see his hands
until now, the rose
materialized there
slight of hand
magic of an actual smile
eyes shaking
he passed it to me

-Baldinger

1942

he left the squalor of a pinched life
for if nothing else
some air
some hope
some change
something

dirt under boots
truck treads
it made even less sense
on the other side
of a polluted ocean

explosions showed
all blood was the same color
when it was on the ground
everyone was the same
when reduced
to meat and memories

he accepted the rifle
thinking change would come
but not this

-Benger

when hope is on life support

there was a planet
on the playground
big and small holes
children pop through
a game of wack-a-mole
the ever-present smell of piss

that planet is gone
no more pisspants
no more brutalist concrete
seventies playgrounds

now people get married here
I've been to a couple
mostly because I always know
the exact right time
to play *purple rain*

tonight, punk rock babies
are taking pictures
of their miata
in the shadow of observatories

a '79 bonneville hangs a left
beeping horns for familiar
faces, time goes out
of focus, it's '83 perhaps

waiting on my father's tan
plymouth fury to turn
around the cul de sac
then wheeze to park

that car was a beast
abandoned to three flat tires
forgotten after his death

my mother finally sold
the fury in '86 for a benjamin
seed pods falling into snow
as the tow truck took it away

it was a cold day
off from school
I shoveled snow
drank hot cocoa

the same kind
of mid-eighties winter
day in the rust belt
when rockets fall out of the sky
and hope is on life support

-Baldinger

sunday

i have only one memory
of dad's canary yellow camaro
which as that one memory serves
reflected the sun
with a greater intensity than
any paint job i've seen since

rare weekend off
dad was doing dishes
in that little trailer
while mom was off
waitressing at pizza hut
my toddler brother was zoning out
to some public access fishing show
on the woodgrain tv
and i was silly puttying
the sunday funnies

garfield was best
he had the score
way better than that
blockhead dingus
he knew what was what
even if he wasn't quite as cool
as that other orange cat
heathcliff

garfield was certainly cooler
than the only orange
amongst the stray cats
i regularly fed on the sly
that cat i'd named biff
in mock honor of the
bully from back to the future

while dad dried the plates
and my brother checked out
some old dude bagging bass
and mom undoubtedly
pour another for a drunk in town
i decided i needed
some of garfield's cool in me

so i tore him off the page
wadded him in as tight a ball
as my tiny fists would allow
and shoved him as far
into my sinus cavity as i could

dad caught me in the act
sighed a tired fuck
a fuck that said
this is my first day off
in a long time

then he loaded us into that
canary camaro

and we flew the gravel
dropping my brother off
at grandma and grandpa's
in town by the tracks
then heading straight for the clinic

tweezers and some blue stuff
in a squirt bottle
that looked suspiciously like windex
were the order
and the newspaper was extracted
and disposed of
and the nurse made me promise
i'd never do anything like that again

back in seatbeltless backseat
i asked dad if we could
stop by the mcdonald's
and get some cookies

-Benger

the hymn to thrift store ties
(for adam matcho)

I was working third key
at an office supply store
it wasn't what I wanted
I was desperate
I spent a year going on an interview a week
hoping for resurrection

I got a call from a book store
I'd been hired at three times before
timing always required me to decline
another job on the ladder
another path paid better

this time would be different
this was to change my luck
I could feel my luck change

I felt good
I thought I should wear a tie today
I didn't have a decent tie
I stopped at the thrift store
picked a dandy off the fifty-cent rack
risked being late to look proper
my donation a prayer to saint vincent depaul
whoever the fuck that is

I arrived, assured
the interview started
the manager and I
dismantle questions for talk
I was charming
I exhibited my wit
my ease with people
I was exemplary
I would be a model employee

he compliments me on my tie
being over honest
I picked it up at a thrift store on the way here
he compliments my taste
maybe he should buy his ties in thrift stores

black friday days away
we completed our conversation
the manager tips his hand
we need a magazine manager you'd be perfect
call monday, we'll get started

on the air
the salt mines of office supply soon shuttered
the holiday ahead, I could be easy
I could enjoy my stay of execution

monday is green grass in november
I shake sleep anxious for telephones
I call, get the runaround

the manager isn't here call tomorrow
now I'm unsure

days pass I'm religious
not convinced I've been jilted
wednesday, someone finally offers answers
the manager had been fired
the day after the interview
they would not honor his last hire

-Baldinger

trajectory

i was wandering the goodwill
as i so often did
of a rare morning off
looking for cheap records
random electronics
clothes without holes

i was figuring this
spongebob t shirt
would fit me
i wasn't into the show
about a decade too old for it
but it was stupid and childish
and sometimes
i needed some of that

i was deciding on spending
two dollars on a
first pressing of
all things must pass
the jacket had some issues
but the vinyl was solid
a few years later
i'd unexpertly giftwrap that album
give it to my then future in-laws
on their 30th wedding anniversary
because my sweet lord
was their song

i was perusing the furniture
when reality punched me in the face
told me a goodwill couch
without bugs
disease
blood
or semen
was about the best
i could ever hope for

-Benger

our great and wasted hours

tonight, I dream
of a bar I frequented
with its giant shark
abominable snowman
its tree branches
filled with silent birds

I miss noise tonight
bar ambience, penn avenue
a stifled staccato soundtrack
to our great and wasted hours

gin and tonic, cold beer
she wears a vintage
yellow dress, floral printed
the one she wore the first
night I kissed her, back
before the carter family
set world was on fire
back when mcclellan's
troops froze under
the expanse of heaven

goodnight stars, cold bloom
rhododendron blossoms fall
tonight, I miss noise

-Baldinger

anonymous

these streets remain
frozen four a m silent
slush congealing at the sides
our nights become sluggish
a knife blade of a new way

the air is a painful reminder
of what it really is
without all of this
without us

we're window dressing
on a world that
never really asked for us
we're the ornaments
that weigh down the structure
destroy the substance
with an overabundance
of useless symbolism

huddled inside
the old records spin
but the needle needs replaced
the notes losing their flavor
under the dust of these moments

singular cars kick up brown water
temporarily painting the
unused sidewalks

frost collects on windows
further encasing us
isolating us

a world in a box
while our hills
reclaim themselves

-Benger

say hello anywhere

watch a beater truck
drive straight into the burnout heart
of a faded burger king sign

this is the chrome plated
plastic center of the world
you can eat, sleep and hunt
among the mattresses, bedding and baptists

the stockyard railcars
leave the lights on
the ice is coming
ice is filling
swollen creeks, drilling pads
everything shines
in a mild psychotropic way

this is the midwest
every road is a candlelit hex
every road is a crossroad drugstore
every road is a tattooed waitress
    sleeved in an abandoned gas station

say hello anywhere
among the motel beer lottery
among the old hanging trees
among megachurches
among car dealerships

the wipers flummox everything
squeaking the rhythm of 5:26
it's winter, everything's dead
desolation across cornfields
sheep drown on front lawns
the new year sleeps in

it's january on the other side of the state line
I see the blackhawk shine
a beacon tonight

-Baldinger

inanimate tears

we're floating in this
endless microcosm,
searching for anything
to bring solace
as we circle a drain
only a few years ago
we would've sworn
was at least a couple
lifetimes away.

acoustic guitars
and sweet folk voices
won't change anything;
they're the spoonful of sugar,
but that cod liver oil's
still gonna go down, by god.

i sit in my truck on my lunch break,
drink a soda,
windows cracked
like i've done on rainy days
for the past fifteen years.
i listen to the new pj harvey
that actually was recorded
twenty-five years ago,
and her melodious voice helps me forget
for a moment.

but the abandoned burger king
across the street
has a haphazard sign in the cracked window,
says:

help wanted.

-Benger

panther hollow lubrication

it wasn't the night security
almost caught him pissing
in a potted plant, it was wild
turkey and pbr, panther hollow
lubrication, mostly competent
velvet underground covers
here comes the ocean

the reverend was blackout
blotto into the wall
outside his apartment
fractured his wrist
a fact hidden till the next day

that winter was mid shelf
bottom shelf tours
the snow would come
the next night
twenty five inches deep

my housemate and I
run the penn ave iditarod
to dj a valentine shindig
down 40th sliding
bail out to an open grocery
if the weather wanted hostages
at least we'd have limes

in the snowdrift dunes
the icehole days to come
no one would come
to the next gallery show
canceled. the touring band
talked about nothing
except jared leto

maybe you don't know this
but leto owns a decommissioned
military base in laurel canyon
not far from where charles manson
was employed by the cia
to kill what *they* call the sixties

decades are decorations
skimmed surface of memories
blurred on a precipice
of collateral damage
and barely keeping shit together
another hangover close at hand

in nicotine and suicide attempts
the reverend was right
don't get your hopes up

-Baldinger

cinder

when all the wires are crossed
what's left to do
but sit down in the
middle of the road
and take stock of all that's left

bloody and unhinged
our lives flap like
the cold fish
freshly flayed
and not far from the pan

nights like this
we hide inside ourselves
hemorrhaging our needs
into a noxious pool
of all that once made us human

none of this makes sense
but it never did
and maybe it's not supposed to
who are we to
put order in a world
that was simply
better off before

we're clinging to some
childish hope that
someday we'll atone
for all that we've caused
bring it back home
and start again

but the circuitry's
rat-nested and dry-rotted
and the only thing to do
is set the whole field ablaze
and start from dirt tomorrow

-Benger

the eyes of the world
(for billy wilder's sunset boulevard*)*

skip tracers
repo men
and the corpses
at the morgue
sing the tune
st louis blues

hey betty schaffer
you ought been told
william holden is a coward
a sideways swimming
slippery fuckin' eel

the eyes of the whole world
knew gloria swanson
they memorized her matinees
she lost everything but her eyes

a microphone drop
shatters depression glass
she never left 1932
a ghost finds voice
a face salome can never forget

three shots
the body slips
staggers into the pool
water turns to blood

she doesn't know it
this moment
is the perfect precipice
the moment before
how much was lost

the last second
before crescendo
before lights
everything still
the eyes of the whole world

-Baldinger

sensory

we're living in a world
of lights and noise
strobing
flashing
and pulsating
in our faces
numbing us
to all comers
all nuance

we're bleeding out
but electricity tells us
keep on
keep moving
this is all for the best

there's nothing
but clinical precision
detaching ourselves
from ourselves
from each other
from our world

we're burning
from the inside out
freezing solid
and losing any sense

of what this was
what happens
when the lights say go
but there's nothing left of us
to move the meat

what happens
when all that's left
is the cold
the sterile

what happens
when the projector plays
to an empty theatre

-Benger

civic arena march 7, 1984

snow on the dash
snow crunches under the tires
of a '77 rabbit, her friend's boyfriend
with a handful of pills to share
she plastered a pint in her jeans
security never looked anyway

into the dark of the floor
fog machine smells
the pills slowing down
speeding up together
diamond dave glitter blur
and fuzz this far away

running with the devil
into *eruption,* she never cared
for long solos but
whiskey and counting
23 times for the word jump
it's infinity… what's infinity?

drunk enough, on her boyfriend's
shoulders, arms up gigantic
as they tore in
ain't talking 'bout love
last song and it's everything
spinning, freedom is a ghost

waiting to go numb
the post office ain't the same
there ain't nothing wild
left of what remains

-Baldinger

Blood

dad sold his blood
on saturday afternoons
a couple times a month

mom off waitressing
or maybe the warehouse job
or any other place the temp agency
would send her
dad'd load us into the
rusted quarter panel conversion van
soup can dangling from baling wire
(i think it was beef noodle)
to catch the constant oil leak
that van where the stray cat died
on the block one horrid january morning
that van he once let me drive home
from cub scouts, only to have
a crow go headfirst into the grille

dad'd back out into the dirt and gravel of
marquette avenue
all beer cans and spent needles
and we'd roll down 41
hoping for potholes, that when hit at top speed
would give you that roller coaster stomach
if only for a second

there was this lot at the side of the highway
lettering on the sign out front

always made me think of jars of miracle whip
they *sold luxury housing solutions for*
our new mobile world
which meant singlewides
and fifth hand rv's

right next door you'd find the tiny white house
rail out front in case you felt faint while leaving
they'd put dad in a recliner
hook him up to red stained plastic tubes
let us sit in the corner
had the biggest tv i'd ever seen
must've been twenty eight inches, and color
gave us orange juice and
oatmeal raisin cookies
tuned the box to *masters of the universe*
while they slowly sucked dad's blood

one time mom and dad took us to the circus
i was afraid of the clowns
but i got a huge bag of
the world's butteriest popcorn
and a plastic cap gun
and I still remember the red stripes
the salt on my winter chapped lips

mom and dad
they gave us those first memories
and they paid for them in blood

-Benger

where are you now benny santiago?
(for tony gloeggler)

improbable opening day
the swelter of july
the fate of the season
the fate of the country
hangs suspended
in this unsafe air

it's been years since
I made it to an opening day
last one so cold
the stadium
voted a campfire
as between eighth
inning entertainment

previous year was shirt sleeves
forty year old benny santiago
whacked a triple
even from the upper deck
you could see his eyes wide
digging for second, spare
parts strewn across the diamond
he slides winded into third

I wasn't thirty yet
I already knew

what that run meant
how each stride felt
benny retired the next day

I look over this year's opening
day roster, selfish I know
the 'rona cost a chance
to see a historically
bad pirates team lose
over a hundred games

I've sat through seasons
like that before
listening every night
a roster of aaaa players
not looking for wins
hoping for attrition

I don't think this season
will ever finish, suspended
in an open ledger like '94
no boys of october
the crisp of autumn
ushered in without ceremony

tonight stallings
the backup catcher
drops a single, brings in two
the bucs never catch
the cards though

they need magic
come the ninth
with a couple runners
on, only one out
they get lightning instead

harmless double play ball
game ends, soon forgotten
stadium lights blink out
the dustbin of minutia

I turn off the radio
settle back into a book
breathing water in humid night
sometimes it's attrition

where are you now benny santiago?

-Baldinger

last night's whisper

most of these nights we blow in
seeing ourselves in shadows
backlit in the oblivious oblivion
of all those wasted hours
the ones that once flashed so brilliant
in the glory of exuberance
now dulled and tempered by time
curled into something more akin
to today's reality

those nights of technicolor love
where we were all
neon anemones undulating
in a fishbowl of blessed acceptance

when shackles were thrown
when bonds were things of history
and overreaching storybooks

when truth floated contentedly
on the breath of fabrication
and all that mattered was
arms around shoulders
and a resignation to youthful righteousness

hair grew freer then
with experimentation the operative word
of every day

when adventure was always in toes
when fingers never rested
and the only thing better than headphones
were the rich kid's speakers in the man cave
while his uncontented parents
were out tying one on
trying their best to reclaim and remember
everything that was happening
two floors below where they would
later lay their heads

those nights everything but death
was upon us
and maybe that too
but low numbers breed an invincibility
now remembered and mourned
but not missed

and books close
while their denser cousins
wait patiently

-Benger

I can't make this akron
(for victor clevenger)

victor, I know you're out there
watching my apartment sink
like the titanic, I know
it's not that dramatic
it's really not even as cool
as getting hit by a streetcar in akron

but you were there, no civilization
in your pocket, watching a dragon
and an octopus and the titanic

I'm sorry I can't make this akron
but in the warmth of the summer
in a time before ice water and unraveling
you watched my apartment sink
as fatalist lovers fucked against
children's home walls

they left condoms in the street
a telegram to pittsburgh
that brief time when we forgot the h

my neighbor remembers
you asleep on the stoop years after
cigarettes and lighter next to you
not noticing the sun
inching through gingko leaves
if she hadn't walked up when she did

maybe that sun would gift you
your own iceberg
your own streetcar

I came starboard hours later
john brown in bathrobe
tossed the deadbolt
you were awake and salty
mumbling about slaughterhouses again

-Baldinger

twelve bar

for Jason Ryberg

it's just them old blues
crawling in
low and slow
sinking everything out
from the bottoms of your feet
leaving you flat

seeing the bare trees
as nothing more than nothing

a '57 chevy
rusting out in the abandoned field
where volunteer berries
almost want to grow

it's just last night's promise
forgotten in an envelope
under all of life's bills
collecting dust
and other particles of
everyone else's existence

it's just your blood
flowing backward
and spiraling into a drain
on the floor of the

truck stop shower
while another nameless body
does their best to erase

it's just a sunset
oranging your light
and threatening nocturnal amnesia

it's just them old blues
so flip the record
there's more

-Benger

once I was

I struggle with a cheap
ballpoint, a handful
of postcards on the couch
in a king sized econolodge
sunday morning room

fog rises, mountains
swallow highways
time moves to new york
or some other place

cary grant just died bloodless
drunk with an ingenue
also dead now, they notice
their corpses, wait on trumpets
realize some good deed
will send them to heaven

I find the remote wrapped
in sheets, take my key
stare at dead lights
an overgrown baseball field
the half tarped empty pool
several boats lost in the storm
of an appalachian savanna

the paris of the northern tier
there used to be music and dancing
every night, prime rib on fridays
I guess we'll always have paris

I watch decades, start car
read a map as a novella
seconds speed. long past
morning glory, well fit for frowsy
once I was, once I was

-Baldinger

claude's brush

we retread past syllables
finding ourselves under
napkins meant for reminders
or secret missives
left under a two euro tip
in a paris café

rain slick soda streets
are bootheels of innocence
a shouting to the universe of future

boozy brothel windows above
and the man under the newsprint
sits waiting for anything

we promise ourselves a tomorrow
as sun flirts with the edges of night
and clouds hang windmill low
threatening easy puncture

suitcases roll cobblestones
on a cold morning
street vendors give overpriced coffee
in miniature paper cups

our a m goodbyes near
smoky tracks through a monet station

pigeons fight wind
while turnstile miles enlarge
and new lives wait in the wings

-Benger

working poor pretend

I didn't have anything
smaller, so I put a twenty
in the dollar changer
at the laundromat

it rained quarters
nearly a full minute
I was rich during that time
all that silver drained out
over a slot machine eternity

this is working poor pretend

-Baldinger

twelve points shuffle

and you staggered out of
the red onion
like some extra from
keroauc or fitzgerald.

aunt suzie gave you
the stink eye
as you pushed the door
open and walked
shamefaced down
into the topless bar
with the big high heeled boot
neon sign.

when i was little,
i thought that sign meant
it was an italian restaurant,
or maybe a knickknack shop
selling indiana americana.

but the look on your face, man,
that look i still remember
all these decades later.

funny how shame,
even someone else's shame
can etch into our bones.

-Benger

regular and subtle as god

(for linzi garcia)

the teleporter plays
hell when it assimilates
atoms that were once
me back into me
just in a different space

no real casualty
but for some reason
where I assimilate
whatever pair of pants
I'm wearing somehow turns
into pants decorated
with red sequins
I'm embarrassed to be seen
in any line of time any other way

although I've managed
to build a transporter
I'm not very handy
I do know we perceive
the universe as chaos
maybe we get a reprieve on
the 43rd sunday of the year

it'll be october by then
there won't be much shade

or any leaves blowing down
sixth street, pumpkins
on the front stoop
won't remember your birthday
they'll listen to train whistles
flow across the kansas night
regular and subtle as god

-Baldinger

tomorrow's chance

everything in our shared atmosphere
when the right mind is
applied directly to the instance

sunday sunshine can give warmth
on the coldest of tuesdays
an internal blazing
through a willful recall of synapse

even the blood trickling
from the rift left by the knife blade
can become last lifetime's
wakeboarding of foaming sun

collective distortion of reality
is often necessary to
reclaim ourselves
for tomorrow's chance

-Benger

spook the horse

the waitress offers
a fifty-cent bounty
on every fly dropped

the cathance river
runs in my head

a pitbull sits
patiently, waits
for any lost scrap

goose island
covered
in halos

one fog
obscures
the ocean

words fat, beautiful
gray, hang over the sky
words like
damariscotta
skadumpha
words that no longer
belong to a tongue

if I close my eyes
I'm lost
in a wyeth painting

rafters of turkeys
cemeteries materialize
from nowhere

buggies wave
along blinn hill vistas
I slow down, don't want
to spook the horse

-Baldinger

another cold one

these are the nights that
give quiet the jinx

the cold blows up
fearsome outside
and the cat in the window
of the town's last video shop
which also sells snacks
which also sells live bait
from a cooler behind the counter
lazes by the radiator
doing its best to
sleep off this life

muffled in the back of everything
is the last lovers'
last embrace
as all falls into an
eternal ocean of indifference

there's a bloody footprint
on the cracked and salted
sidewalk out front
but there aren't many
who would pay that much mind
as anything that's not grey
is something to be praised
no matter the cost

snow and ice hide what's left
of the water tower's paintjob
but that means nothing to
the dog's tail's last night of
aimless twitching

they rent nudie flicks
behind the beaded curtain
and that's the most civilized thing
this night could hope to provide

-Benger

our temporary time

in the weeds
of another year ended
feeling like the ghost
of dennis hopper
feeding a raccoon
pancakes hot
off the griddle

I knew a woman who
told stories of raccoons
salt water taffy
and junkies running
the hallways
of the ohio river
abandoned

this isn't about dennis hopper
this isn't about trash pandas
junkies or persons who lose
themselves in the mazes of their mind

this isn't about bob kaufmann
or the working class
both are dead

this isn't about the ohio
carrying microplastics
to the mississippi
to the ocean

it's about abandon
how I miss the ocean
how we deserve the ocean

lights blink out
across the consciousness
of this organism planet

I think of the ocean
its temporary roar
matching
our temporary time

-Baldinger

ocean

we stood on the edge of everything
waiting for next seconds
as tides rushed and slouched
their own patterns
answering to nothing
but the wind
howling in the ears
of anyone willing to listen

we wondered what it would be like
to join the tide
in eternal acceptance
and the future
pulled us
to wherever
we ended
up

-Benger

ask the dunes

the cattle call said
wait ninety minutes
for a steak
in the deadlights
with no bar
a clown car parade
somewhere in the car park

this is not homecoming
it's nostalgia. seasons
conspire in the dark
something like temptation
in green neon windows
this was a safe space
for underage drinking
now, no one cares again

I'm going to the ocean tomorrow
ill freeze before breakers
fight with or against tradition
i'm still not sure
ask the dunes

waiting in line for day old bread
furniture has glass city remnants
no one knows when jesse james
is in town, or why he's leaving

the valley of work is silent
braless in the streetlamps
when I pass the next cadillac
the snow will fall for minutes
that's what left of winter

if the gas station is open
get a night cap
madness never retires
grace yaps at the front door
all it takes is a key
in the door to remind
all this is temporary

-Baldinger

stream

we would always
return to the stagnant
tadpole water
under that bridge

spent rubbers and beer cans
the scent from the neighbor's grapevines
would offset the sewer runoff

it was a freedom
beneath everything
and we saw ourselves reflected
distorted and murky
something inside ourselves
under the water
living amongst the
bacteria of a neglected ecosystem

knives were traded
with bloody abandon
and tales grew longer
as the water went maroon
with the sinking sun

cars would crunch the gravel overhead
and we pondered
what it would be like

if the old cracked concrete and steel
finally gave out
and we were ended
under someone's failed joyride

sometimes that morbid fantasy
seemed almost preferable to
ever surfacing again

-Benger

Jason Baldinger is from Pittsburgh and misses roaming the country writing poems. His newest book is A *Threadbare Universe* (Kung Fu Treachery Press), as well as the forthcoming *The Afterlife is a Hangover* (Stubborn Mule Press) and *A History of Backroads Misplaced* (Kung Fu Treachery). His work has been published widely across print journals and online. You can hear him read his work on Bandcamp and on lp's by The Gotobeds and Theremonster.

James Benger is the author of two fiction ebooks, and three chapbooks, two full-lengths, and coauthor of four other split books of poetry. He is on the Board of Directors of The Writers Place and the Riverfront Readings Committee, and is the founder of the *365 Poems In 365 Days* online workshop, and is Editor In Chief of the subsequent anthology series. He lives in Kansas City with his wife and children.

www.ingramcontent.com/pod-product-compliance
Lightning Source LLC
Chambersburg PA
CBHW022014120526
44592CB00034B/809